IN THE SLEEP
of
RIVERS

JOSEPH STROUD

I
N
T
H
E
S
L
E
E
P
O
F
R
I
V
E
R
S

Joseph Stroud

Capra Press / 1974 / Santa Barbara

Drawings by Tom Thompson

Some of these poems appeared in the following publications to
whose editors grateful acknowledgement is made: *Choice, Cloud
Marauder, Guabi, Kayak, Sundaze, The/The Anthology.*

ISBN 0-912264-98-5 (pa.)
ISBN 0-912264-99-3 (cl.)

Capra Press, 631 State Street
Santa Barbara, California 93101

To the Memory of My Mother
Roberta McNamara Stroud

TABLE OF CONTENTS

PART THREE *How Came Beauty Against This Blackness*

Part One

HEART, YOU HAVE NO HOUSE

> *Such is my heart's own stuff. I can renew*
> *Myself with images of broken trees,*
> *The coarse delights of an unfaltering rage.*
>
> *Heart, you have no house.*

THEODORE ROETHKE

WORDS FOR A SUMMER DAY

In the sleeping dead of summer
I scratch my name on a cloud.
I can hear the skeletons of insects
Crumble in a dry wind,
And crayfish in the pond
Raking their claws against sand.

The dust of a thousand summers
Trembles in my mouth.
Leaves of dead trees flake in the sun.
Who can tell what the grass is saying?
Weeds are whistling through my hair.
Fish cry in the streams.

I want to hide in the cracks of trees
Away from the worms who plot my death.
Away from the meadowlark with its blue tongue.

Somewhere a hollow dog barks,
Rolls over,
And listens to dragonflies
Weaving patterns in the summer air.
I tried to touch a sorrow
When blackbirds filled the sky
With yellow eyes.

Tomorrow I will love.
Today I will sit here
And count the faces on my hand.
I will sleep
And dream of the berry patch
Where crickets weep quietly in the leaves.

GRANDFATHER

Now I see you
In a small California town
Asleep under fig trees, the black fruit
Swollen and ripe. Your shadow seems
To deepen on the morning grass as peppertrees
Scatter their leaves like rain
Or seeds.

I remember a summer morning
We sat on your porch, the warped boards
Pocked with holes and nails. The fields
Freshly cut. The pond rimmed with willows
And magnolias. You tried to tell me
Why my brown bitch had eaten her young.
It was a morning of bees.
I saw the light sing on their wings,
A mellow gold quaking into music.
You must have heard too
For when I turned you had fallen into a dream,
Your throat humming with veins.

Then I heard that other music. The cicadas.
The green frogs. My bones
Drained like the sap of trees
As I dreamed myself into the heart of the pond.
I forgot everything I ever learned.
Except your voice. Down there.
Singing of home, death, a blossoming tree.

IN THE HOUSE OF SILK

When I was a boy
I dreamed in a house of stained-glass wings.
Each morning was a summer of listening:
The soft-tongued birds outside my window.
The opening flowers. I would lie in bed
And watch a breeze rustle the curtains.
I promised myself never to touch the words in my throat,
So my brothers never knew who I was
When we climbed the hills behind our house.

Once I spent a whole day
Crawling through rotted leaves and ferns.
I came upon a clearing
Where the sun laced some white-lipped ivy
And gold pollen eddied like snow
Into the center of a spider's web.
I knelt until I found her
Nestled against a leaf, face sparkling with eyes,
Each skinny leg cramped under her
Like crooked children at suck.

I wanted her to come out of the dark.
So I stabbed my tongue
Through that thin carpet of silk
And drained from the moist threads
The inner gleamings of a spider's heart.
She would not come out.
I think she knew the flesh that tore her home
Had no wings or eyes.
Or perhaps she felt the sudden cries of bees
Swelling in my throat.

That night, my brothers asleep,
I rubbed my sticky fingers under the pillow,
And dreamed of women with silk hair,
And those small, needled mouths
That sewed my lips with kisses.

THE OWL

for M.C.

When I think of you
I hear the owl.

I remember the night we slept
In an old farmhouse by the highway
And how the long, slow drone of trucks
Filled that room. We heard an owl shriek
And found it next day, near the road.
You said, "That owl died chasing beams of light."
Then you cut off the talons
And hung them on a piece of leather
Around your neck.

We sat for a long time
Beside the road, listening to crickets,
Thinking of owls and how they are always
Exactly what they seem: the yellow, lidless eyes
Of the dead we all feel in us.
I can't even look one in the face
Without realizing I have a beast
In me. Or a woman.
I thought of my grandmother's eyes
When she covered me at night,
And her smiling, owlish face.

The sun grew warm under our skin.
Along the ribs of the valley, sprinklers
Showered the alfalfa fields with a sheen of silver.
It was a Spring morning. And we
Were never the same. You followed the light
Of that year to your death. And I
Went away to write or sleep
In the rich spools of leaves under the trees
And found myself singing into an owl's dark voice.

LOVE SUITE

for Georgiann

1.

The tall grass is quiet.
I sit in a green prison
Dreaming of the lost years of my face.
Across the meadow a red-wing blackbird
Sings to his mate. He is
A blossom of music on a thin stalk.
Alone,
No one shall hear our throats
Move like water over stone.
Gold.

2.

I wake with the moon rising
Outside my window. In my dream
I was an evil man. But now
All the leaves in my garden spill
Into silver coins.
In the blue shadows of a cedar
I see moss honeycombed with faces.
I am in love. All night I wait for morning,
The earth full of windows,

3.

She stands at the top of the stairs
In a white dress. I remember
A night I spent my love
Looking
Up the long, dark trunk of a tree,
And seeing, at the top,
How the tangled branches broke open
The moon's treasure.

4.

I have climbed this tree
Before. Once
It was full of leaves, heavy
With apples and gold light.
But now it is raining, the tree
Uprooted, and utterly gone.
The earth is open at my feet.
In my mouth
The taste of moonlight.

5.

Two butterflies dip
Through small pockets of the wind.
They weave chaotic patterns, yet
Beautiful, this dance of love.
See how they touch, once, over the reeds
Of a pond. Just so
We move through our lives
Knowing
We do not touch easily.

POEM TO MY FATHER

Always
Always
Always
All ways I see are dark unto stone.
And if I should kneel in a field,
Shirt open, the sun on my shoulders,
Knife against my wrist,
Calling down black birds who shall love me,
Who *shall* love me? Father, let me sing,
Though blind, my eyes draw from yours
The light of age, poverty, a spirit
Looking for wings.
                    I took myself into language
Believing all the fables: the talking beasts,
The forests that rise and walk at night,
Until I felt all the world in me
Heave loose, fall
And fall deeper than dreams
Into dark. Alone, a room to myself,
I shaped my life into an ark. Ocean
Of silence, deep water, I want to love.
Father, let me learn, make me see
Our lives together. I am your flesh
As you are mine. Let us walk
Close to the earth.

POEM ON THE SUICIDE OF MY TEACHER

We are the bees of the invisible—RAINER MARIA RILKE
The secret lies in the egg of night—LOREN EISELEY

1.

No moon No road No thunder
A white tree with black veins

Give me the ocean repeating the movement of my blood
Give me the bell that wakes the woman who bears the earth
Whose flesh is fruit split open to the moon
Whose life is a net of blue fish
Give me the strength of a root
For we've been hung on our ribs to die

Let my wound grow Round as the sun
Let me return my life to the spine of the stars
Let my language come home to its nest beside God

I am the wife of night
My throat falls with snow
My hands are a puzzle of water
My life bells like a candle plume

2.

Gordon is dead. Where
Do I place my grief? Lord,
It is time now. I hear a skull within a skull weeping.
I see the perfection of death.
It is a monkey claw at the throat of the moon.
I listen to my blood. Tonight.
The stars tell me nothing.

Mystery. We explored it in lab. The cadaver.
You naming all the organs, tissues, muscles, bones.

I saw your hand kneel in the chest of an old man
And raise out his shriveled heart.

"This is unreal," I said. And now
Your death is inside my head
Like a fist, clenching.

3.

Teacher
You gave me *The Immense Journey.*
So what was your own? Its end
Takes me to an abandoned road when I was 9 years old:
A meat truck with its back doors sprung open,
And emerging from the shadows in the back,
Two cops holding between them a man
With his throat cut open, the blood gushing
In heart bursts. I entered another kingdom
That day. A railroad bridge where I used to climb
Under the beams among the pigeon nests.
I cradled in my hand a thin, blue-speckled egg
As a train screamed over the tie-bars and rails,
Darkening the light over me, until it simply
Disappeared. Dust sifted onto my hair,
Onto the broken, drooling egg. I wept.

4.

You are the son of a bitch that broke the circle
Around the house that kept the flame
To feed the sons you left
To bear your death.

May their lives quicken into blinding mirrors.
May they find some help on their own dark day.

5.

You move away, Gordon. Tomorrow you will be less,
And less each day. Until only your wild Irish grin
Will glimmer, silked, webbed in memory, that spider,
The mother of my language that recalls
And calls you: Teacher Alcoholic Suicide

What kind of breast or egg were those bottles
You sucked on? Even the final image. A shotgun
Among the digs. Among the scattered bones and beads
Of Indians dead for centuries. So what
Was your final lesson?

The earth of Soquel is black in Autumn.
The corn stalks are dry, withered old men.
This morning I dug a grave for a rabbit.
Each shovel I gouged with fury, and grief,
Thinking the earth was your chest,
Hoping to wound your dead heart. To find it.
To open a vault in you, as the one in me.

BELIEVING IN THE DARK

for Michael, my twin brother

In the last breath before sleep
I dream of summers beyond the dead
Where the sun moves in a shadow beneath my eyes
And takes the shape of tongues.

Here in my summer home
I listen to the foxes in the bone
Beckon the moss to climb trees in moonlight.
Everything has a beginning in dark places.

While watching swallows skim over black ponds
I understand there can never be the real,
Only horses grazing in the meadow
With their sloped backs trembling
And the scars crawling on their legs
Like wild snakes
Where barbed wire has opened the blood.

Here, at the edge of my life,
I lean to a song in stone.
When I touch water
There is a dancing in my hands.
All my life has come to this.
Alone, in my own dark,
I sing back to water and stone.

Part Two

THE VOICE I HEAR

The voice I hear this passing night was heard
In ancient days by emperor and clown:
Perhaps the selfsame song that found a path
Through the sad heart of Ruth, when, sick for home,
She stood in tears amid the alien corn . . .

JOHN KEATS

Monte Alban
                    In the ruins at night
Lights in the valley of fires

The wind among the stones
Fireflies flickering over the ground
In the mist
And softly under those small lanterns of light
Illuminations
The tarantulas moved
                    Ghosts of black hands through the ruins
Oaxaca Oaxaca

ISSA'S LAST JOURNEY

What can I say?
My life has come this way before.
And suddenly I hear the bells
From inside the mountain.

POETRY: A KIND OF BONDAGE

As a boy, Rilke kept two pet squirrels
On long chains
So their freedom ended only in the light
Of the upper branches.

BYBLOS

I entered the field
Where the cow lay on its side
A crater into its stomach.
And inside, thousands of worms
Writhed and boiled,
A sound like the pure whine of generators.

I saw, clearly,
The ruins of my city.

POEM TO HAN-SHAN

Often in this life
I think of you—
Marriage broken, sick of the world,
Making the treacherous journey to Cold Mountain.
You came closer than any of us
To stone, stream, cloud,
To the pearl of the mind.
30 years alone with silence,
Cliffs,
Your laughter and tears.
The Governor who expected wisdom
Sent his aides ahead
Bearing gifts and medicine.
O Han-shan, screaming "Thieves! Thieves!"
Before you disappeared
                    Into the mountain.

LAMENT

Because the moon became my mother
No need to weep
Because the tree broke open its honey
No need to weep
Because the blade always finds the heart
No need to weep

CANCIONERO
> *for Oralia*

I want to listen to you
For when you speak I hear
The green music of strawberries in the wood

I want to be with you
Before the leaves turn to gold
And violets bleach to a valley of bone

I want to touch you
For your fingers are the throats of candles
Your mouth is a cloister of water

TO CHRISTOPHER SMART

I will praise Christopher Smart
For his life was a flame unto the Beloved
For he wrote with a key on the madhouse wall
For he slept in class and taught in the tavern
For his secret name was Mother Midnight
For he knelt in the street and asked strangers to join him
For he sang out of poverty and debt
For he saw the Lord daily and drank with him often
For in his nature he quested for beauty
 And God, God sent him to sea for pearls

HARVEST:
THE FARMER AND THE POET

Four times a year
My landlord comes with his tractor
To plow the orchard.
In Spring he imports bees to excite the blossoms.
In Summer he thins the apples.
In Fall he sprays against aphids and mold.
In Winter he prunes the branches.
He does this to keep the trees alive
And to insure a proper harvest.

All night through my sleep
The moon sails across the orchard,
And invisible worms,
Like words,
Glow in the throats of the trees.

FUCKING

Like in Lascaux
Where the cave tunneled back into the heart
Of the mountain.
Men brought their fires
And shaped on the walls
The totem beasts of death.
Re-birth therein.
Magic in the prick of paint
In darkness. The dream
Swells. Outside the day
Bloomed. The creatures fell.
Spears in every throat.

ON THE RIB-BONE OF A COW

In the gradual curve
                    of the rib
The lucid architecture of death.

_____

Inside the hard bone
The marrow is honey-combed.
                            Small, secret chambers
Of dark bees, death's honey.

_____

Where the river went dry
This rib
            stark white
                        in a bed of stones.

_____

Who could have known?
The simple, stupid heart
                        of cows
Encased by curving swords.

_____

The Angels, splendid
                    in their white flames,
Fail
    before the elemental touch
                            of bone.

_____

One curving rib,
                imagination's white wing.

THE WONDER OF IT ENDING
IN THE WORLD

for *Ellen*

The heart never fits the journey.
Always one ends first.
—JACK GILBERT

I think ahead to that moment
Silence has prepared for me
When I shall look back
And sing
How all that year we lay together
In the field through the nights
As the seasons colored us
As the trees blossomed
And the berries ripened into Autumn.
Our small, white house
With its windows and music,
The monkey in the roses,
Your serene, gracious love
That opened my life.
And I gave my heart
As my heart broke down,
O my love.

CRAFT

Careful. As stone.
The tower out of the air.
Like mountains. Perfect.
As in love. Dolphins.
The landscape etched
In me. My heart.
That room in Taxco. High
Near the thunder. The light
Cracking the white walls.
Alone. Of myself
Without want. My people
Gone from me. The years
As stone. Full of care.

THE YEARS

All week
The boy has crouched in the field
Picking off meadowlarks one
By one
A dead bird
For each year of his life
He will never
Get back

POEM TO HAN-SHAN (II)

I've come to the age
When you abandoned everything—
Wife, home, and friends
To begin the solitude of Cold Mountain.
I've come all these years to this
Ignorance, this failure
To complete even the simplest of things.
Each day I begin.
By night I am stunned back
To the empty page,
While others, casually,
Build their house.
I come finally to the orchard,
Drunk and naked in the rain
Being led home by a girl.
Cold Mountain
Cold Mountain
Is inside me.

PIECES

for Duncan Holbert & Charis Wilson

King
Look to him.
Impotent. Helpless.
A cross on his life
And nowhere to hide.
You will never take him.

Queen
The bitch. And the Goddess.
The taker. Furious
With power. We all fear
Her touch. Trap her
And the game is over.

Rook
Rock without heart. Castle
Of the clear road. Straight
As light. Hard.
In the end, the King
Loves you best.

Bishop
Deceiver, always working
The angles. Sly and quick
As God's word in flesh.
A prick over the pawns.
Worthless on the same color, the same faith.

Knight
Even the Masters
Do not master you; for man,
That poor, bare, forked animal
Loses his own beast
In your hooves, your strange movement.

Pawn
All of us, our life
As days— pushed, sacrificed,
Worked, and dying. Our hope—
Re-birth, the animal heart
Transformed on the last rank.

TRAIN

adapted from Miguel Hernandez' *El Tren de los Heridos*

Silence
Trainwrecked into silence.
The profound roads of gold
Like murdered ruins, like trains,
Without the voice of the sea.
The invisible train in the blood.
The fragile train of anger,
Grieving Pale,
The long train of agonies.
Love train of the empty heights
Where the dust of the heart
Sweeps across the stars.
The white train of desperation,
Fear of red steel, smoke
Of the father, the engine
That advances its sorrowful cargo.
The long mother of the tunnel
Where the stations of the heart
Are abandoned hospitals.
The destined train of death
That shrills in the cruising night.

LUPINE

1.

I came into the years
With you, mother,
And now I must endure the silence
Of these early, February flowers.

2.

Death like rain
Washes us clean.
Mother, is it so?

3.

Mother, no
Word of mine
Shall find you.

INUKOK

How dare we make the poem,
To think our language could manage
The strict, literal heart,
While everywhere around us
The earth,
Alien and fatal,
Flowers into paradise.

CALLIGRAPHY

In Calgary
I saw a man break a dog's back.
Leaves on a white hill.
The moment as ideogram
I cannot translate.
The absolute, actual tree
Shames my life.
And Pound singing how splendid the words,
Like marble,
Persist through time.
Virtu in the vortex of death.
Calligraphy of what the seasons leave
To the mind.
The city in the heart
In ruins.
The dog broken in the street.
White hill.
Leaves.

EXILE

Hommes, ici n'a point de mocquerie;
Mais priez Dieu que tous nous vueille absouldre!
                                    —Francois Villon

Ten years Villon lived in a small village
Outside Paris. Often the Pastor
Watched him walk from the square
To the graveyard under Gallow Hill.
But no one saw Villon steal the Eucharist
And eat the wafer in his dirty room
With the peasant girl, half-dressed,
Mindless in the heat, sweating and moaning
Under the sentence and law of that Medieval light.

Part Three

HOW CAME BEAUTY AGAINST THIS BLACKNESS

But the beauty is not the madness
Tho' my errors and wrecks lie about me.
And I am not a demigod,
I cannot make it cohere.
If love be not in the house there is nothing.
The voice of famine unheard.
How came beauty against this blackness,
Twice beauty under the elms—
      To be saved by squirrels and blue jays!
              EZRA POUND

A DREAM OF FLOWERS

In Vermont I climbed the wooden fence
Beyond Skeets Pond Road
And walked in a field of flowers.
I wanted to find something. A horseshoe.
A chunk of shell. Pale, blue eggs. Some
Thing I could hold in my hands.

When the wind came up
I crushed a tunnel through the thick green vines
And flowers. The smell of broken stems made me drowsy.
I put my face to the ground
And sucked on the sweet meat of mint.
Falling asleep I thought I could hear
The dead breathing of beautiful horses
Under the earth. In my dream I saw flowers,
Their mouths opening and closing
Like delicate jaws.
The long, soft teeth
Runneled with small veins.
The blood thin and clear.
Jewelweed and adder's tongue, they swarmed
Around my throat until I woke.
Clouds moved across my face.
It was all like breathing.
Or drowning.

POEM TO WELDON KEES

These speculations sour in the sun.
I have no daughter. I desire none.

1.

But you have a son, Weldon,
One who has followed the arches
Of bridges and music
Hoping his dream of fish
Would swallow him whole.
In Mexico he loomed in the fire
Of every bar
Drinking to the hope of your shape
Half expected, lean
And tough as the cactus
Whose juice drowns any Fury
For a time. He found you
In cattle thin as the blades of machetes,
In a brown Indian carpet
Chewed by the chalk-blue moths of age.

2.

Was it through that dog of bones,
His furious gold eyes,
And the scent of pine at night
That I remember your life?
The owls thrashing in the needles.
The cave you opened,
Following that hurt
Where the mountain sucked cold air.
There were no fish.
Only bats with pinched faces
Streaming the light from your hand
Back at you. Where the worm
Ate its life out of the ground,

A single eye at the mouth
Blind as the finger
I point at your death.

3.

And that is the lie of the poem
Weldon. The imagination
Like a snake swallowing the literal world.
It was not the lushing turn,
The road that loops back upon itself,
The crabbing dance of spiders
That killed you. A slow
Realization. The phone
Hooked to your ear like a pincer,
The human voice amplified
Three thousand miles, all
The connections plotted.
The stunning electric hum of our world.
The spirit soldered
And plugged into the very walls
That separate us,
The Furies made physical at last, atomized,
Radiating over the earth like a cloud.

POEM ON THE DAY OF OUR INVASION

The performance we wait for
Defines us its attendants
—ROBERT DUNCAN

1.

Today our dead dream above earth.
They lunge stakes in the river
And sing of the goat's white bones,
Of the heat that blisters the corn.

Our President winds along the edge of a gorge.
He can't see the bottom. From his hands
Dangle puppets. The strings
Are *moon silk* he tells us,
And he lowers the figures like live fish,
A blade hooked in each of their throats.
The performance is for something deeper
Than our sight,
Untouchable,
Mute.

2.

This morning
We wake to blue light in white rooms.
To wind chimes
And hummingbirds jeweling the lilacs.
We wake to each other.
All our promises are fire
To this moment, to what we can receive from it,
If love, if *anything* would grace our life.

We strike the flame from windows
And burn our flight of ashes.

Still the war hangs its iron calendar around our throats,
The walls begin their long skeleton.

3.

Who can begin the field, the green
Bleedings of earth, the owl
And his pool of light?

Who can clothe his love
In the light of a language
That would open in us
The crown of touch?
Let him tell us about the moon again.
The dead moon that robes its light
Around the horse that leads us out of life.
Let him sing clearly of the hawk
That translates its shadow over the earth
Until all things plunge deeper into holes.
Let him begin.
For we attend the falling of mountains,
The grave of the sea.

FOR THE MARINES WHO COME BACK FROM THE WAR
A CHANT TO STRING THEIR BEADS

As part of the therapy for those
men who acquire a taste for battle
in Viet Nam, some Marine psychiatrists
have them weave baskets or string
beads before they re-enter society.

One world to begin the song
One song to make a mountain
One mountain as a sermon
One sermon to feed as fish
One fish to wear the sea
One sea to reflect the light
One light to flame the curtain
One curtain to wrap a dream
One dream to restore the thorn
One thorn to prick the truth
One truth to marry the head
One head to bless the grave
One grave to close the night
One night to bleed the stream
One stream to open stone
One stone to weight the hawk
One hawk to nest the egg
One egg to feed the snake
One snake to coil on death
One death to blind the stars
One star to fashion love
One love to redeem itself
One self to start the fall
One fall the hope of touch
One touch the world begins

THE GARDENER, SLAUGHTERING SNAILS

They toil in the forgotten places of the earth.
All morning he gathers them,
                    slithering his blind arm
Into the dank foliage and slick tendrils of ivy. His fingers
Like bloodless worms
             grovel in hairslime and holes.
Occasionally they bring back a pair plugged together.
These he throws into fields,
              feasts for shrikes and jays.
He packs a paper sack snail-full, builds a fire in a barrel
Until heat blisters the paint,
            then hisses them into flame
Listening to the flesh foam and ooze
And the furious explosions of shells.
                  All day he hunts.
In the geraniums around the gutter of the house,
Under stones, the cracks in boards.
              He seals a plastic bag full of them
And holds it to the sun. They bubble in their green juices.
These he will sling from a car,
             splatter on a back road.
Looking through the bag, he thinks of his garden.
The fuschias and roses. The order.
             He knows there are thousands
Sealed in holes,
Cradled in the blooms of his lilies,
             waiting for night, for sleep,
When they come out with the stars
And silk all his petals
            with the slime sheen spittle of the moon.

POEM TO BARTLEBY
BEGINNING WITH A LINE FROM TU FU

Tumult, weeping, many new ghosts . . .
Shall we enter? Let me open the door
For you . . . The room is no larger than our death.
I know the peace you seek is without
Language. Only the act is important. A tree
Grows many lives, many ways to begin
The Fall. I know there are songs to be believed
In time. Your past became your present.
The wall crumbles. In time
The heart opens, the words come.
What are you to throw all beginnings
To the dogs? To that man with fat hands
Who brought you soup? To that cold, glass canopy?
I prefer not to ask what you mean. Old
Ghost. Father. I hate the truth
Of your story. How long do we go on
Suffering each other? I reach
The distance I began ten years ago.
The circle. The dance within the stone.
The flame that keeps the motion pure. Christ,
Bartleby, your story is just another
Myth. God weeps in you. Your walls
Were more than stone. They would not
Fall, would not burn like Autumn.
I know there are many myths.
I own none of them. My own
Begins here. Where it should. In the
Beginning of a line that goes through me
To the stars I wish that you could see.

THE PISCES TO THE IGUANA

Where must I come from?
Through what ocean or jungle
Have I watched my claws turn to hands,
My skull to expression?

At some flickering point
You must remember. As in a dream
I see your emerald skin, its crest
Of spines flowing down your back,
The turquoise head and gold-flecked dewlap.

How else shall I describe you?

If I could, I would make you understand
What you are to me. How my poems
Keep you in mind. Your black, gold-ringed eyes
Looking somewhere past
Or beyond. We are as different
As brothers.

DIPTYCH

1. *The Beast*

Our bed is a white tongue in the mouth of a closet.
She sleeps in the cage of her breathing.
I crouch over her and think of the beast
That dreams in my blood. How he has stalked through me
Like a thin river
And fed under the root of my love.

                                  I know
His lust turns my fingers to small moons of touch.
That nothing can kill him. He is with me
When I open a closet door
Or walk down blind steps to the cellar.

                                    He is here
Facing this slow breathing dreamer
                                   Waiting
For her eyes to open.

2. *The Woman: Testament*

We lie in the dark.
                            I stroke your hair
And recall a forest; slow, insect days
Of crawling through bushes, slipping my arms
Into leaves, thrilling

At the touch of bark. There was an animal
That ravaged the cave in my dream. The moon
Turned his horn to foxfire.

I want your hands to make miracles of roots.
I want you to shape those trees, that beast,
Into the language of my flesh, your voice breathing
Like a wing. Tonight

You opened the closet door, loosened
The screws, and rolled the bed onto the floor,
Then touched, and burned, and wept

Until the wooden mouth swarmed
With the blanket smell of roots and holes,
Dark moss, rain. I want to ask of your tongue
A gift to bring this beast we grow between us.

ENTRANCE

Why are you out there?

This day's so hot
The shade is shriveled, a dead tree
For cats to sleep under.
Like you, old man, my land
Lord. I will not come out to your voice
Through the screens. I hear it
Calling.
It begins from the hole in your back
And whistles through your teeth like a sail in winter.
Oldness. Your life's time.
I see you snarl vines into barrels, choke
Weeds, and sweat, murdering everything
You've not planted. You're so old
I have to pay you to live
Here. You built this house.
Let the weeds grow!
I want to say let the earth take
Over. It's April. I'm twenty-six. Oh
Fuck it. I'm coming out,
And I will bring you a glass of cold wine.
I *know* what I am.
I will bury the cats beneath your shade.

SPRING IN THE SANTA CRUZ MOUNTAINS
WITH LI PO

Here, our life
Is the absolute clearness after rain.
We sit in the middle of a path
Near an acacia tree.
Under a rush of branches
Where the stream pools,
A towhee dips its feathers
Shuddering water into jewels of light.
A squirrel shrills in the scrub oak.
She is furious we have come
To her throne of leaves.
We hear the long drone of a wasp
Far off
Near the sun.
Bees brush the brilliant clumps
And yellow powder
Of acacia blossoms.
You say,
"It would be lovely to taste their ecstasy,
Or be that pine tree,
My limbs spread out, a living, glorious crown."
This place is so many tongued.
Blackberry vines wander through sage.
A strand of web
Like our thin filament of love
Spins the sunlight
And laces it into small rainbows.
It's no use to think here.
We are not important.
An ant tugs at your sandal
And the wind rises.

It is all beginning, Li Po.
Dusk,
Mountains,
And the rivers
We hope to become.

POEM TO TU FU

Tonight, drunk as your friend Li Po,
I dream of wheat in a white vault.
I cannot imagine your jade flower palace,
Nor the war thousands of miles away.
It's been a long summer.
In my garden a bullsnake rules a weedless throne.
The monkey I keep for wisdom has learned to tend my heart.
Today I washed the shed, tore the nests of spiders,
Poisoned wasps, and painted old boards.
Summer is cruel, old man. It is like our poetry,
Taking from us most of our silence,
An easy life, a few friends. So we drink
To boats and mountains, to whatever gives back
The strict moon or green stones
As our fingers open a treasure of seed.

from PRAISE POEMS

For John Logan

To the Day
    For it begins our journey—
    It is the mountain
    Over our homes

To Water
    For it is the way of the spirit—
    We are blessed
    With its invisible wings

To Fire
    For it is the voice of God—
    It is the bright color
    Of all our children

To the Horse
    For it leads us from this life—
    It runs in darkness—
    It bears us across the waters

To the Bear
    For it sleeps beyond death—
    It follows the bee's
    Trail of pollen

To the Father
    For he leads the way—
    He is the hand of shelter—
    He bears our grief

To the Mother
    For she gives us to the world—
    She is the happiness
    We find in ourselves

To Salt
    For it comes from weeping—
    It is the Saint's pearl—
    Our touch of stars

To Morning
    For it is the open door—
    It is the welcome
    Of all our friends

To the Grass
    For it is the blade that does not cut—
    It is the joy of our sight—
    Our green marriage

To the Stars
    For they are seeds of light—
    They are the small, pure songs
    That rain upon us

MEMORY

for Tim

It is dusk
On the bridle path that wanders
Through the Griffith Hills.
Two boys walk, arm
In arm, under the branches of oak,
Madrone, and pine.
They are brothers going home
Before the sun goes down.
Walk with them. See
How the smaller, younger one
Stretches his stride to keep
Beside the other. They
Talk quietly
Having spent the day for snakes
In the hills behind the bales of hay
Slit with arrows the grown-ups shoot
For sport or hope. Why
Do they stop before a tree
Swarming with bees?
In the gnarled roots they see
An emerald lizard with spines
Down its back. Don't wake them.
It's no dream as they dream
A kingdom to allow such a beast.
Crowned and golden, they continue
Home, a sound of bells,
In the huge, quiet night.

IN THE SLEEP OF RIVERS

for Tom & Jimmie

1. Roots and Stone

Beneath the steady field
Beneath the dry roots descending
A river sleeps in stone.
I feel that dark under me
Pulling at my breath and bone.

A hawk's eyes turn
Above the moist tongues of grass.
Shadows bleed into moss.
A bluejay screams
In the upper branches of a redwood.
They've learned to listen
Into the voice of rock-rose.
But here it is the night of water.
Leaves dangle like pale roots.

In this air that blisters the heart,
Pinecones crack open, seeds
Twirl
And fall over ferns and stone.
My seed is blown
Over the breathing pores of blackberries.
Now the bitter fruit will sweeten,
Swell, and drop heavily among weeds.
And where the pungent sperm spoils in the sun
Bees will swarm their honied mouths.

In a thicket of tangled roots
Where mushrooms swool from the skull of a deer
And the hawk-torn beast crawls home to die
I opened a river in stone.

2. Russian River

Alone,
In the evening I sit by the river's edge
And toss stones into the shallows.

The river is silent.
Deer make their way
Across a ridge on the mountain.
A hawk rises into the clouds.
In the closing leaves, a blessing,
A rustle of small bells in the wind.
This land was not meant to sing.
There's hunger in the cold trees.
Colors no law defines.

At the end of a season
I wait for the poem I've always waited for.
It does not come.
Even here
Clouds move slowly under the stars.

3. Face in the River

Night
I make a fire out of dry leaves
And stand over it, watching
A dance move in the flames.

The moon comes out of the clouds.
I want to see its veil of light
On water.

Kneeling, face
Over the river,
I do not understand my life.

The face, moon-swollen,
Strange,
Carries its own shape
Down
To the tips of grass
Streaming in the current.

I want to go down
Deeper than the sparkle of moon.
Something in me
Wants to breathe water,
Fill my lungs with ice,
Sleep in the dream of trout.

4. A Dance of Rivers

The morning is in clouds.
To close my eyes now
Would have the mountain down on me.
A lover. Limbs for tongues.
I follow my hands
Up a trail glazed by deer.
High over the hills

I gaze across the valley
And see the river join the ocean.

And I remember another river,
Another summer in Vermont
Where I swam into the deep
And let the current
Take me down among the rushes and waterbirds.
On that slow journey
With the shrill cicadas and bronze dragonflies
I flowed through a joy deeper than years.

I give myself to this memory.
Waves curl in the river's mouth.
The sun burns through a deep haze.
I begin a dance, and the lips of shade
Part to my dancing.
As the hawk turns slow above me
I move in the sleep of rivers,
While beneath my feet,
Deeper than the roots of trees,
A river moves through stone.

*Designed and printed by
Noel Young for Capra Press
in Santa Barbara, March 1974.
50 copies have been handbound by
Karen Meece, numbered and signed
by the poet.*

JOSEPH STROUD was born February 23, 1943 in Glendale, California. He received his B.A. in English Literature and M.A. in Creative Writing from San Francisco State College. Since 1968 he has lived in Santa Cruz County on the California coast where he teaches English and Creative Writing at Cabrillo College.

192800

"Poems of clarity and compassion"—George Hitchcock

"*A poet who writes with beauty, and who strikes to the memory of us all, and the hope.*"—John Logan